TIMELINE OF PABLO PICASSO'S LIFE

1881 — Pablo Picasso is born in the seaside town of Málaga, Spain. The style of painting known as Impressionism is just starting to become popular around this time.

1895 — Pablo studies art in Barcelona.

1897 — Pablo goes to Madrid to study art, but leaves after a few months.

1900 — Picasso travels to Paris, France, the art center of the world at the time.

1901 — Pablo begins his Blue Period paintings.

1905 — Begins his Rose Period paintings.

1907 — Picasso discovers African art at a museum exhibit. The simple, mysterious wood masks and figures inspire many of his works. He and a few artist friends begin to develop Cubism, one of the most important movements in modern art.

THIS WAY

UP HERE

1914 — World War I begins.

1917 — Picasso travels to Rome, Italy. He gets lots of ideas from ancient Roman sculptures he sees there.

1937 — The small town of Guernica, Spain, is bombed during the Spanish Civil War. Picasso begins *Guernica*, one of his greatest works.

1939 — World War II begins. Picasso continues working in France.

1955 — Picasso is now super famous. He moves to Cannes, on the French Riviera. He creates tons of new paintings, ceramics, and sculptures. He loves entertaining famous people from all over the world.

1973 — Pablo Picasso dies at the age of 91 in his large hilltop home near Cannes, France.

GETTING TO KNOW THE WORLD'S GREATEST ARTISTS

PABLO
PICASSO

WRITTEN AND ILLUSTRATED BY MIKE VENEZIA

CHILDREN'S PRESS®

An Imprint of Scholastic Inc.

New York Toronto London Auckland Sydney
Mexico City New Delhi Hong Kong
Danbury, Connecticut

To Pat and Gene with love

*The author wishes to express a special thanks
to Sarah Mollman*

Cover: Boy in Sailor Suit with Butterfly Net. 1938. © 2014 Estate of Pablo Picasso / Artists Rights Society (ARS), New York

Library of Congress Cataloging-in-Publication Data

Venezia, Mike, author, illustrator.
[Picasso]
Pablo Picasso / by Mike Venezia. — Revised Edition.
    pages cm. — (Getting to know the world's greatest artists)
Includes index.
  ISBN 978-0-531-21976-8 (library binding) —
ISBN 978-0-531-22537-0 (pbk.)
  1. Picasso, Pablo, 1881-1973 — Juvenile literature. I. Title.

ND553.P5V35 2014
709.2 — dc23
[B]   2014014727

SCHOLASTIC, CHILDREN'S PRESS, and associated logos are trademarks and/or registered trademarks of Scholastic Inc.

2 3 4 5 6 7 8 9 10 R 24 23 22 21 20 19 18 17 16

Pablo Picasso was one of the greatest artists of the twentieth century. He was born in Málaga, Spain, in 1881, and died in France in 1973.

Picasso's father was an art teacher
at the local school. He encouraged his

son to paint and draw. He wanted
Picasso to become a great artist
some day.

The Altar Boy. 1896. Canvas.
Spain, Courtesy Abadia de Montserrat, Barcelona

Picasso's painting style changed
over the period of his life more than
any other great artist. He was always
trying new and different things.

The painting above was done when
he was only fifteen years old.

Boy in Sailor Suit with Butterfly Net. 1938.
© 2014 Estate of Pablo Picasso / Artists Rights Society (ARS), New York

This painting was done when Picasso was fifty-seven.

There's quite a difference between the two paintings, isn't there?

Girl Before a Mirror. 1932. Canvas, 162.3 x 130.2 cm. New York, The Museum of Modern Art

Sometimes Picasso would paint
things that looked very flat.

Bather with a Beach Ball. 1932. Canvas, 146.2 x 114.6 cm.
New York, The Museum of Modern Art

Sometimes he would paint things that looked so round that you might be able to pick them up off the painting.

When Picasso was nineteen, he left Spain and went to Paris, France. Some of the first paintings he did there look a little bit like the work of other famous French artists.

This painting reminds many people of the work done by Toulouse-Lautrec. Some of Picasso's other early paintings remind people of Van Gogh, Gauguin, and Monet.

Le Moulin de la Galette. 1900. Canvas, 90 x 2 x 117 cm. New York, Solomon R. Guggenheim Museum

11

THE BLUE PERIOD

Then something happened! Picasso's paintings changed. His work became different from anyone else's.

His best friend died, and Picasso felt alone and sad. At the same time, none of his paintings were selling, and he was almost starving to death.

Because of his mood, Picasso began to paint with lots of blue (blue can be a very sad color). He made all the people in his paintings look lonely and sad.

The Old Guitarist. 1903. Panel, 122.9 x 82.6 cm. The Art Institute of Chicago

Some people thought Picasso's blue paintings were great. Others (including Picasso's father) thought they were just too strange. This meant his paintings were controversial.

THE ROSE PERIOD

Picasso's Blue Period ended when
he met a girl named Fernande.
Fernande and Picasso fell in love, and
soon a happier color started showing
up in Picasso's paintings. This was
the beginning of the Rose Period.

Family of Saltimbanques. 1905. Canvas, 212.8 x 229.6 cm. Washington , D.C., National Gallery of Art

Not only were Picasso's colors happier during the Rose Period, but he started painting happier things. Picasso painted a lot of circus people during this time. He often painted them with their animals.

The Rose Period didn't last very long, though, because Picasso found a new way to paint that was really exciting and different.

Portrait of D. H. Kahnweiler. 1910. Canvas, 100.6 x 72.8 cm. The Art Institute of Chicago

CUBISM

Cubism was the next style of painting that Picasso developed and made famous.

This is a cubist painting of one of Picasso's friends. The man in the painting looks like he's been broken up into little cubes. That's where the name cubism came from.

Look closely. Can you see the man's face, what he was wearing, his hands, a bottle, a glass, and maybe his pet cat? Can you find anything else?

Portrait bust of Eugene de Beauharnais, viceroy of Italy (1781-1824), in military dress. Salon of 1808, Gérard Blot. Oil on canvas, 39 x 32 cm. RMN-Grand Palais / Art Resource, NY.

Cubism is one of the most important periods in the history of modern art.

For hundreds of years, artists tried very hard to paint things so they would look real. Then Picasso came along and started to paint people and

Weird.

Woman with hat, Pablo Picasso. 25 November 1942. Oil on canvas.
73 x 60 cm., Bridgeman-Giraudon/Art Resource, NY/ARS, NY.

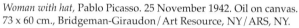

Hmmm. I think they're getting their noses out of joint over nothing.

things that didn't look the way
people and things were supposed to
look.

Picasso was always shocking
people, but when he started painting
people who had eyes and noses in the
wrong places—well, even some of his
closest friends thought he had gone
too far.

21

Picasso kept working with cubism and changed it over the years. It became much more colorful and flatter looking. It also became easier to see what Picasso was painting.

In the painting *Three Musicians*, you can see the three musicians, and tell what instruments they're playing.

In another style that popped up for a while, Picasso painted people who looked more real again. Picasso had

Three Musicians. 1921. Canvas, 200.7 x 222.9 cm. New York, The Museum of Modern Art

Three Women at the Spring. 1921. Canvas, 203.9 x 174 cm.
New York, The Museum of Modern Art

just visited Rome, a city filled with
statues and monuments. When he
returned from his trip, he did a series
of paintings in which people look like
they've been chiseled out of stone,
like statues.

GUERNICA

In 1937 something happened that made Picasso paint his most powerful and serious painting.

During a civil war that was going on in Spain, the small town of Guernica was destroyed by bombs. Thousands of innocent people were killed or injured.

Picasso became very angry and used everything he knew to make a painting that would show the world how foolish war was. He named the painting after the town that was destroyed.

Guernica. 1937. Canvas, 351 x 782 cm. Madrid, Museo del Prado

Picasso used darker colors, cubism,
and lots of expression to get his
angry feelings across in this painting.

He also used size. This painting is huge. It's 12 feet high and 25 feet wide!

Portrait of Jaime Sabartés as a Spanish Grandee. 1939. Canvas, 46 x 38 cm. Spain, Picasso Museum

Many of Picasso's paintings look funny because of the way he moves eyes, noses, and chins around. The amazing thing about these paintings is how much they look like the real person.

Look at the painting of Picasso's best friend, Jaime Sabartés, on the opposite page. Does it look like the same man shown in the painting below?

Jaime Sabartés, painted by Steve Dobson, from a photograph by Gilberte Brassai

The thing that made Picasso such a great artist was his originality. He had the imagination to try new and different things through his entire life.

The Ape and Her Young. 1952.
Sculpture. Paris, Musee Picasso.
Giraudon/Art Resource

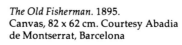

The Old Fisherman. 1895.
Canvas, 82 x 62 cm. Courtesy Abadia
de Montserrat, Barcelona

Minotauromachia. 1935.
Etching, 49.2 x 69 cm.
The Art Institute of Chicago

Weeping Woman. 1937.
Canvas, 60 x 49 cm. London,
The Bridgeman Art Library/Art Resource

Four Children Viewing a Monster.
1933. Etching, 33.5 x 44.8 cm.
The Art Institute of Chicago

Picasso lived to be ninety-one
years old. He was a great painter, but
he was great at other things, too.

He made sculptures, prints,
drawings, beautifully colored dishes
and bowls. He even made costumes
and scenery for plays.

It's a lot of fun to see real Picasso paintings. You'll be surprised at how big some of them are. Look for his paintings in your art museum.

The pictures in this book came from the museums listed below. If none of these museums is close to you, maybe you can visit one when you are on vacation.

Abadia de Montserrat, Barcelona, Spain

The Art Institute of Chicago, Chicago, Illinois

Musee Picasso, Paris, France

Museo Nacional Centro de Arte Reina Sofía, Madrid, Spain

The Museum of Modern Art, New York, New York

National Gallery of Art, Washington, D.C.

Picasso Museum, Barcelona, Spain

Solomon R. Guggenheim Museum, New York, New York

LEARN MORE BY TAKING THE PICASSO QUIZ!

(ANSWERS ON THE NEXT PAGE.)

1. What was Picasso's favorite spectator sport?
  a Monday Night Football
  b Bullfighting
  c Ping-pong

2. Picasso's middle name was:
  a Randy
  b Kevin
  c Ruiz

3. Which one is a famous Picasso saying?
  a "Every child is an artist. The problem is how to remain an artist once we grow up."
  b "OK. Where did somebody hide the leftover pizza?"
  c "One if by land. Two if by sea."

4. **TRUE OR FALSE:** Picasso sometimes mixed expensive French perfume into his oil paints to attract more buyers.

5. Picasso had a pet . . .
  a Bull
  b Dachshund
  c Madagascar hissing cockroach

6. **TRUE OR FALSE:** Picasso collected old broken objects and trash to sell to junk dealers because he was saving up to buy a new skateboard.

7. What kind of food did Picasso like?
  a Puree of salted codfish
  b Frog legs
  c Grilled eel
  d All of the above

ANSWERS

1. b Today, many people feel bullfighting is a cruel and unnecessary sport. But some people in Spain feel it is an important part of their history and culture. Picasso made many paintings, prints, and drawings of bullfights throughout his life.

2. c Actually, Ruiz is just one of Picasso's middle names. When he was born, his parents named him Pablo Diego José Francisco de Paula Juan Nepomuceno María de los Remedios Cipriano de la Santísima Trinidad Ruiz y Picasso. In Spain people named their babies to honor their parents, relatives and saints. Picasso's parents probably wanted to make sure they didn't leave anyone out.

3. a Picasso believed all children can create pure, simple, and beautiful art because they are free from all the busy responsibilities that can clutter grownups' minds.

4. FALSE Picasso never added perfume to his oil paint. But he did cut out printed cloth, newspaper, wallpaper, and other items and glue them to paintings. These works are called collages. Picasso and his artist friend Georges Braque invented collage art around 1912.

5. b Picasso had a pet Dachshund named Lump.

6. FALSE Picasso actually collected old broken items to use in creating surprising new sculptures.

7. d Picasso enjoyed Chinese and Indian dishes, as well as salted fish, grilled eel, Stilton cheese, frog legs, and much more. He liked to try all kinds of foods.